The Cone of Uncertainty

The Cone of Uncertainty

Poems by

Lucile Burt

Kelsay Books

ISBN: 13-978-1-947465-52-7

Kelsay Books
Aldrich Press
www.kelsaybooks.com

in memory of my mother and father
Betty and Gardner Burt
with gratitude for their love of words

Acknowledgments

I wish to thank the editors of these publications in which some of these poems appeared, sometimes in previous versions:

Altadena Review: "The Plague of Squirrels"

Bacopa Literary Review: "Lake Ontario"

Prime Time: "Kayaking the Upper Pamet in May"

Provincetown Magazine: "Tasting the Fruit from the Tree of the Knowledge of Good and Evil"

Red Rock Review: "One Summer" and "Saving the Turtles"

the Atlanta Review: "Postcard Not from Santorini"

the Lunar Calendar: "Eclipse," "Moondial," "Night Walk II" and "Winter"

"Saving the Turtles," "Someone Loved Returning," and "What They Feared" appeared in my chapbook *Neither Created Nor Destroyed,* winner of the 2012 Philbrick Poetry Project Prize and published by the Providence Athenaeum.

My appreciation to Truro Center for the Arts at Castle Hill, Noepe Center, Queset House at the Ames Free Library, Wellfleet Public Library, and the Brewster Ladies' Library for providing wonderful workshops and space for these poems to come to fruition.

For Mark Bailey, gratitude for teaching me the patient art of rock balancing and for the spectacular cover photo of the rock he balanced under an eclipsed moon at Halibut Point." (Find his work at www.markdavidbailey.com)

Thank you to the Narrow Land Poets—Leo Thibault, Wilderness Sarchild, Donna O'Connell-Gilmore, Chuck Madansky, Marjorie Block, and Dianne Woods Ashley—as well as former members, Susan Webb, Barry Hellman and Paula Erickson, for careful and thoughtful reading of these poems. And to Keith Althaus, whose workshops were helpful in re-working many of them. Special thanks to Lorna Knowles Blake for her brilliant workshops in which some of these poems were generated, and for her helpful suggestions for revision. And thanks to Ani Finch for wise guidance and support in shaping the manuscript, to Nancy Volksen for careful reading and copy-editing, and to Gabrielle Griffis for help in formatting. Finally, thank you to my dear friends who have encouraged me always. You know who you are.

Contents

Drift

Dried pods of butterfly weed
split open, spilling bursts
of silky filament, each
ferrying a speck of seed.

Briefly the air fills
with floating bits of fluff,
fragile and lovely as hope
adrift on the whim of wind.

Few will fall on fertile ground,
rest in winter-cold earth,
burst forth in spring
in some unexpected place.

From one small brown seed
packed tight with bright gifts
for monarchs and honey bees,
the orange surprise of survival.

The End of an Ordinary Day

Inspired by Earth Alive, a painting by Cis Rossey

We are the still point, sitting
at the bar on the bay.
Plate of oysters. Glass of beer.
The setting sun spreads
on the horizon like a broken yolk.

But if, for just a moment, we hold
the sun as fixed, then we might feel
how bar, beer, oysters, shore, bay,
we ourselves, are all spinning
together east into twilight.

Harder: the slow roll of summer
to winter, tipping us away
from light. Our only guides:
shortened day, slanted shadow,
sun riding low in the sky.

Impossible: our sun and planets
swirling in the Orion Spur
at the edge of the Milky Way,
the galaxy a tossed disc flung
away from the cosmic center,

the whole universe flying apart.

We finish our meal, walk out
in our illusion of stasis
into spinning dark
scattered with near stars.

Someone Loved Returning

Even if all those we ever loved,
leaving, went lightly,
and we knew they would return,

even if we recognized them when they came
as hurricanes or cardinals,
and we could speak
the language of weather and birds,

even if we had the patience to wait,
listening, and let them come
in their own ways,
however terrifying or trivial,

and when they came, we forgave
history and old hurts, willing
to hear their howl or song,

even if we knew we ourselves
would return as reeds or beetles,
forgiven for our whispers and hunger,

even if we saw in every tremor,
every saxophone wail,
every stone rolled by waves at our feet,
someone loved returning,

would you and I, now,
meet like the horizon at twilight,
dark and open, edges blurring?

Walden, October 2001

On this perfect autumn afternoon,
I sit in a tiny patch of sunlight
creating a small boat of driftwood.
On it, maple leaves and a candle.
I sing a song and send it,
fragile and tilting, onto the pond.

My mother's body was already gone
when I arrived this morning—
whisked away for research,
her practical plan, helpful and frugal.
Only a husk, I tell myself,
trying not to think of saws.

There is no ritual for this
in our family of lapsed Christians.
No one to say what must be done,
no funeral director, minister,
no service to plan, no body to bury,
no neighbors delivering casseroles.

The water dances with light.
This is no river. There is no
fierce boatman to row her over.
Only my little boat, carrying
my pagan prayers for her
drifting into dazzle.

Saving the Turtles

for my father

When I could not save your life,
I saved instead box turtles
and endangered terrapins,
who, driven by instinct
to the egg-laying place,
ventured onto risky pavement.

When I gathered them in my hands,
gingerly, to avoid a nip,
they retreated in their shells, not knowing
with what gratitude my hands
lifted them to the other side.

At home, the nurse's hands,
more sure than mine,
ministered to your final needs,
turning you, massaging your heels,
combing your hair, even though
you had retreated inside, your eyes
fixed on something beyond the ceiling.

You were so light, your skin
a thin covering for bone, that I imagined
I could lift you, light as a turtle,
carry you safely to the other side.

Kingfisher

in memoriam Beeby Pearson, 1939-2015

The last image I have
is you at the edge
of your marsh, lying
in a zero gravity chair,
comfort for the skeletal
bird body you had become.
You were listening to birdsong
and smiling up at the blue
sky of May and a circling
turkey vulture. "Not ready
for you yet," you joked.

Mid-summer, far from home,
I sit in the garden
of a sunken courtyard
surrounded by windows,
each a patch of sky.
You are two months gone.
A bird drops near me.
A kingfisher, stunned
and still stunning, feathers
the blue of spring sky.

He lifts off, crashes again
into another lie of sky,
and then again, four times,
until I am so undone
that I wrap him
in my shirt, try
to carry him, safe
to the pond's edge.

I feel his heartbeat
flutter slightly—then
stop.

This is the Last Time

for Phyllis

This is the last time
I will make art
out of your dying.
Don't tell me
"it is what it is."
Just for a few lines
I want it to be
what it isn't.

No eyelashes growing
into your eyes.
No skin sloughing
from hands and feet.
No swelling ankles.
No bone aches.

In these lines
you are dancing
in a purple dress,
swimming naked
in Duck Pond
in moonlight.
Or just sipping coffee
from a blue mug,
reading a book,
gazing out a window.
Even paying bills
or waiting in line
at the market,
any extraordinary
ordinary thing,
heartbeat and breath.

In these lines
that is what is.
Now and forever.
Amen.

Night Walk III

I walk alone accompanied
by winter's bright stars
that may be dead by now
their light still coming to us.

Are you out there released
from the body into star stuff
lighting my way
in the indifferent dark?

Whale Watch

When three humpbacks glide close
to our idling boat, we watchers
go silent,

cling to the rails, hushed by
giant synchronicity.
The whales

undulate a dignified dance
like slow waves rolling.
They rise

and blow, flow below the surface
rise and blow again, a chorus—
whale breath

the only sound above the low
chortle of our engine.
When they dive,

just before I turn away, one whale breaches—her whole body
arcing backward out of the water.

     At the top
          of her leap,

                                    a brief stop
               as if resting on air a moment
            defying her weight and the laws
     of gravity

before she smacks down hard on her back,
                           disappears.

In her wake, the others burst up together
as if for sheer pleasure.

                        I join
                              their soaring.
Their white ridged throats flash side by side in sunlight before
they collapse,
        slap the surface,
                subside
into the sea.

They arch their backs, slowly
tip their signature tails,
dive deep.

I sway with the boat's gentle rock.
My heartbeat slows.
My mind

empties in the presence
of mystery.

Williams Pond

The kayak cuts a swath of clear water
through lily pads that dance
and settle. The pond is dying

in a loveliness of lilies. And its dying
becomes the dark still water
where electric-blue dragonflies dance.

All around the shore, autumn's dance
of vines and leaves spectacularly dying
reflects in the small mirror of clear water.

Water—transforming the dance of dying.

Cormorants

The black-robed amen choir
stretches clerical-cloak wings,
lifts heads proud in praise:
for the deep dive into darkness,
for the burst up to surface light,
for the fish, the full belly,
for sun or rain, for wind drying feathers,
for this congregation.
Amen. Amen.

Winter Solstice

Our voices are nothing
to the sun.
Our meager magic,
even atomic fusion,
doesn't hold a candle
to that burning.

Once, on days of dying light,
men and women danced
around fires on hilltops.
On every high place,
flames leapt, small lights
in great darkness.

A chorus of chanting voices
called back the sun.
And the sun returned.
By their pre-Copernican power,
by their voices, one, around the fire,
they brought back light.

Even now, on December afternoons,
with light slipping away,
if we listen,
an old chant sings in our bones.
From our deepest sleep, a voice rises,
calling back light.

Forcing Narcissus in January

Their heavy scent fills the room.
Deceived by water at their roots
and the thin light of winter sun,
they send out shoots
into this wrong season.

The green shoot does not know betrayal,
does not retreat into the bulb.
The bud does not refuse
to open—its perfumed blooms,
a brief display that dazzles.

To the flower, a simple yielding
to water and light,
to quickening at its core,
the impulse to bloom
into whatever is offered.

Winter

The golden horn of the waxing crescent
pierces the horizon at twilight, sinks
into the bay pulling down the dark shade
of star-scattered sky. Crystalline air
settles over us, carrying the scent
of frost riming the landscape.

Invisible trees creak and sing like ghosts,
ancestral voices that call us to dream.
Without her light, sky surrenders to sea,
becomes a vast round darkness, winter's womb
where everything rests, waiting for fullness,
for the coming fruition.

Entropy

Each year, the old cottage
fades further into gray.
Windows boarded, it turns
a blind eye to the yard,
where plants do as they please.

In March's monochrome,
daffodils startle near
a post lamp, never lit.
June, roses big as fists
sprawl over the porch rail.

Thigh-high wild grasses thrive.
Once someone lived here and
planted bulbs and bushes,
mowed the lawn, pruned roses,
turned on the light at dusk.

Given their heads, plants want
to take over. Spilling
seed, seeking sun, they push
for space. Any frail thing
gives way.

Encounter

In April's still-winter woods,
I meet a solitary tom.
He is a splendor—iridescent feathers,
azure head, crimson wattle and snood.

No other female in sight,
he practices seduction on me.
Tail fanned, feathers fluffed,
wings dragging, he doubles his size.

This act is familiar—
the bulked up muscles,
the sleek hair, the fine rump,
the slow rolling walk.

All winter, at the gym,
he bench presses, checks himself
in the mirror, waiting for spring
to preen in tee-shirt and jeans.

Even if we are years beyond
procreation, our minds turn
to mating, the way spring
wants us all to reproduce.

By Beltane, we're all aflame
with it, the conspiracy of life.

Kayaking the Upper Pamet in May

Come along and float
just inches above the muck,
dense with death and life,
on water still frigid from snow melt
and days on end of April rain
that reached cold into our bones.

Come along and thaw
in air thick with the chorus
of bayberry blossom, first leaves
of swamp maple, birch, scrub oak,
of fiddleheads unfurling,
of red-winged blackbird, yellow warbler.

Thick too with old longings
rising in our chests,
like the ancient snapping turtle
stained with river tannin
fringed with algae,
surfacing for another spring.

Meteor Sapphics

August midnight, Perseid showers starfire.
Sparks in my peripheral vision make me
think of rising. Jump from the rooftop. Fly to
      Cassiopeia.

Just as when I watched from the window dreaming
while my father shot Independence fireworks
into darkness. Now in the silent hours, I
      listen for starsong.

This is that song coming through light years laughing,
sound that's barely audible, waves that ripple,
rolling pebbles, cosmic susurrus. Softly,
      Perseid singing.

The Zen of Physics

North Point, Block Island

You are trying to balance one stone, something improbable.
Heavy base of granite rolled smooth by the sea. On top,
a triangle that stands on a point. You are asking
stones to speak to each other while you listen
with your hands. A slight tilt. A tiny turn.
Millimeters matter. Also patience. You
are listening for atoms to coalesce
where stones meet, waiting
for the triangle to center
on its axis and stand.
You are barely
holding on,
then,
not

.

Weathervane

The old copper goose,
mottled with soft green patina,
fell from the roof in a storm.

She spins now in the garden
perpetually taking wing,
going nowhere, save

round and round like stray
thoughts, turning on themselves,
unable to lift off.

Waiting for Them to Alight

In September, at the Chapman Elementary School in Portland Oregon,
thousands of migrating swifts descend into the chimney at dusk.

At your desk, words flit
like swifts swirling
over the school's old chimney
where they roost at dusk.

At first, a few hundred
make wide circles.
More join with each pass.
Thousands, a dark cloud

that might spin forever,
unpredictable as fleeting thoughts.
Darkness gathers. You nearly give up
waiting for them to alight.

Finally, they form a tight funnel,
flow like smoke reversed
down the chimney—words
settling at last on the page.

Lexicon

White is the dread of what might fill the space.
Space is the miniscule holes in old lace.

Strange is familiar that's heading toward blind.
Blind is a trick of the eyes on the mind.

Soft is the memory stone has for sand.
Sand is the way it all falls through your hand.

Slumber is fruit getting ready to fall.
Fall is a hammer. Winter an awl.

Puddle is moonlight cast on the ground.
Ground is what's moving without any sound.

A Walk in the Woods, October 1991

for Jake

I look up at loblolly pines.
Feathery tops flourish
against a cerulean sky.
I say the name aloud,
a chorus of rolling o's and l's.
Spindly naked trunks rise
above oak, holly, sumac, maple.

The toddler teeters in wordlessness,
squats to observe a caterpillar.
"Wooly bear." I touch it
so it rolls in a ball.
He laughs at this magic,
then dashes down the path,
careens into leaf shower.

I stand still, locked in
the pretty prison of language,
my love for the rhyming chant—
holly, loblolly, wooly bear,
each thing in a word box.
Jake whirls a dance of delight
in a world of nothing named.

Vision

for Peter Elbow

He can see with both eyes, he says
though one goes east, the other west.
Sometimes, he closes one,
narrowing the field to see

what we see. What is out there
on the peripheries,
at the edge of vision?
Does he see

with the horse's bi-lateral sight,
paddock in one eye, prairie in the other,
bridle and wind,
fence and freedom?

Or with the dragonfly's kaleidoscope
of sky, water, predator, prey, cloud,
reflection, rainripple, sundazzle?
Can he see

cruelty in one eye, mercy in the other,
shackle in one eye, key in the other,
brick and wrecking ball,
stone and kite?

When he offers his vision to us,
we try it on, go dizzy from the breadth,
and the missing center,
where we so comfortably live.

Sunday Drummers

We practice rhythms born
in West Africa, carried in muscle
memory of slaves. Forbidden drums,
they played anything—hollow logs
and cooking pots, sticks and cowbells,
gourds and bones, their own bodies—
clapped hands, slapped chests bellies
thighs cheeks, smacked lips, snapped
fingers—music familiar as breath.

In the diaspora, with ecstatic rhythms
known in their bones, they called
their orishas to these new worlds
where they morphed
into Santería, Candomblé
and the secular sound
of *samba, salsa, son.*

We try to learn with our heads
the polyrhythms they knew by heart.
We count beats, read charts,
trying to lay down 3 over 4,
with an off-beat bell, a syncopated
dununba. We can't keep track
of the downbeat. The song collapses.

When we finally give up trying,
we slip out of our minds.
The disparate beats sink
into our bodies. Our hands
move without will, on and on
until a wild tight rhythm
takes us.

Moon Drummer

in memoriam Phyllis Kutt, 1947-2012

The full moon brings her back.
Each month, we see her,
the moon drummer now,
rising out of the sea.
Carrying the frame drum moon,

she dances all night across the sky—
a kiss in passing for Cassiopeia,
a kiss of silvery light for us,
her lovers, standing on the shore
where her shimmering path beckons.

We turn our faces to her
just as we always did.
We step into her reflection,
float on waves of her light,
just as we always have.

A Walk in the Words

I whistle my mind home.
Mostly she's a good mind.
She trots close, sits at attention,
willing to please.
Stay, I say. *This poem*
is what we are doing now.
We are not….

      thinking of new shoes
           (maybe red sneakers)
      or a shopping list
           (lemons, bread, figs)
      or that taxi ride a decade ago with…
           (what was his name?)

Come, I call again.
This poem! This poem!
Pointing to the page, pen poised.
She cocks her head,
hears something move
in a thought thicket,
chases after it, then
after something else,
each calling with equal urgency—

      a fall from a tree at six
           her mother bringing ginger ale
      a hawk stalking chickadees at the feeder
           that's nearly empty (should she fill it now?)
      still air thickening into rain
           the whole coast sloughing into the sea.

Night Walk II

Whatever is in the sky
on a calm night,
the pond holds true.
Tonight a gibbous moon
The dark path
winks with her light.
I go alone,

hungry for something
I can't name.
I hold that hunger
like an empty bowl
I could fill moon-
silvered water
and drink refreshed.

A fish breaks
the glassy surface
as if she might feed
on light she's splintered,
as if the moon might
nourish not her belly
but the need to shine.

Lake Ontario

One night in a summer storm,
my mother awoke to waves
at her window. When a fish swam past,
she woke my father. They fled,
holding high two sleeping children,
as waves broke at their waists.

In my mother's dreams,
did the lake flow into the cottage,
where my brother and I,
fetal fish, swam in the womb
of the living room?
Did she, carrying another
in the lake of her belly,
dash to close windows,
barely keeping her head
above water?

Did she wake, come to us
in our sleep, touch our hair,
testing for dampness?
Did she move outside
where moon-silvered waves
lapped quiet and distant?
Did she stand safe at lake's edge
watching for rising water
while her children slept,
dreaming our dry dreams?

Awakening

When my father died, I wondered
how anyone could die in June
surrounded by so much blooming.
Now I know.

How many seasons
can we give ourselves
to such green pleasures
knowing how it ends?

Each year spring demands more.
There is comfort in cold,
in a scentless white landscape.
I can hardly bear March stirrings.

Until—I throw open the window
to the shrilling chorus of peepers,
perfume of turned earth and lilac,
dance of dandelion floss on wind,

teasing caress of warm air
on skin so long untouched.
A shimmering seduction.
I give in again.

Here's Rhubarb for Remembrance

This garden planted
over the old beds
dug decades ago

by my mother now
a medicinal trove
for any ailment:

purple coneflower
against infection
its burry center

food for chickadees,
sky blue star blooms of
borage (for courage)

once added to wine
to make men merry,
valerian for sleep,

elecampane for
clearing lungs, Joe-Pye
weed tossing tall stalks

tassel-topped globes of
tiny mauve flowers
a cure for fever.

These replace her peas
and tomatoes, this
medicine grown from

her ashes dug in-
to earth she tended.
Only her rhubarb

survived my uprooting,
comes up early spring,
puny and tough, just

enough for a small
taste of remembrance.

Letter to My Sons and Daughters
on All Hallows' Eve

You ask why I let all of you
slough away
month after month until
the end of sloughing.

You want to show me
the peacemaker, inventor, curer.
I saw instead
the assassin, the thief,

the woman with matted hair
mumbling in the street.
I know the short circuit
that spirals in our DNA,

the brother a mother's grief,
the aunt the death of the father.
I couldn't risk
all that breakage.

Oh it was never conscious,
the way I let each month pass.
Just that all your possible
fathers were more evidence

of what could go wrong.
You want me to see
that whatever I gave birth to
can't replace what I did not.

I say it now. I see.
Silence your accusatory chorus.
Too late for a different road.
Under the bright moon, I offer

cakes and wine for your journeys.
Go now. Peace.

For Great-aunt Clara

From the summit of Mt. Norwottuck,
the spine of the Holyoke Range
undulates soft curves of green
lush as reclining nudes.

You stood here silent as the hawk
floating at eye level, seeing everything,
while at home, your sisters
chatted over coffee and canasta.

Were you fleeing the secular convent of home
where no idle moment allowed a woman alone
dreams risky as moonlight,
where busy hands kept the devil at bay?

The faithful novice, you improvised
quilts from scraps of old silk ties,
painted precise still lifes of bowls and statues,
set the table for dinner.

Here, the range lies below like a lover's back,
hills rise like bodies entwined
under a vast green quilt patterned of sun and shadow.
Your breath rapid from climbing,

hair caressed by wind,
nothing above or below you but air,
you must have stood just here,
so very close to the edge.

Clockwise

We don't tell time
on our digital clocks.
Time tells us,
flashing each second.
Staccato minutes show
the instant 9:44 ends.
9:45 begins.
It is never quarter to ten.
Nothing turns clockwise.
Time has no hands or face.

But on the old mantel clock,
wrought iron curlicues frame
a face, hands gesture the hours,
time ticks an audible rhythm,
roughly even, like a heart.
Myriad gears spin
time in slow circles
one minute hour day
flows imperceptibly never
ends becomes the next.

Heading for Darkness

inspired by the painting Night Grass by Kirk Goetchius

1

Winter trees are silhouettes on a snow field.
Afternoons are dim in the slanting sunlight.
From the window, I watch the shadows. We are
heading for darkness.

2

Crude oil runs in rivers on beaches, slicking
over water, reaching its fingers into
birds and marshes, mindless as death, reminding
where I am going.

3

Drones drop bombs on villages, stealthy terror.
Blood streaks walls and floors there, while I sit watching
wintry trees in faraway silence, knowing
I am a killer.

Bones

The Vietnamese believe the unburied dead cannot rest.

On daily reconnaissance missions,
the chopper pilot flew over the same paddies,
hovered briefly over the one
where a dead Viet Cong soldier decomposed.
It doesn't take long in the tropics.

In a matter of weeks, he swooped down
to carry off the skull and two femurs.
Decades later, we don't want to hear
this story on the radio as we drive to work.
We think we have buried the skeleton

of craven acts to which boys were driven.
We do not want to imagine
the way whirling blades flattened thin shoots,
the way villagers fled.
We do not wish to disturb old bones.

The pilot never said why he stole
those bones and carried them home,
to remember—or forget.
His children shrank from the box
gathering dust on a garage shelf.

When he fled to Venezuela,
was it memory or forgetting
or only a wrong heading
that sent his bush plane
into a dense green mountain?

The widow and children waited
for someone to bring his body home,
waited to put his bones to rest,
while in the garage,
boxed bones whispered and moaned.

Bridges

Bedsheet greetings
fly from each one
red paint
name and rank.
Welcome home.
Safe.
Unless
you imagine
how ghosts
from memory
billow and furl
like sheets
flung onto fences,
blood letters
on white ground.

Death of the Enemy

In June 2006, US bombs dropped on a house in Iraq killed Abu Musab al-Zarqwari and his spiritual adviser Sheik Abdul Rahman and four others identified only as two women and two children.

Maybe a woman was chopping
onions for dinner, another
slicing a melon and singing
to two small children playing
on the floor. In another room,
maybe the men waited for dinner.
Maybe the spiritual adviser
was praising the student for good work
in Allah's name. Maybe they were hopeful
about tomorrow, that many
would die in a market bombing.

Just before the first bomb fell on that house,
perhaps the late afternoon sun
slanted through palm fronds, bathing
the rooms in fringed light. Perhaps
the last words were a quarrel
or something about the bread or
the health of an elderly neighbor.

These were really bad guys,
we are told as if we are children
watching 1950's cowboy shows,
as if we might not remember how
the men embraced hatred like a lover,
might not remember the beheadings,
the roadside bombs, the vests
laden with death.

We know the names of the men.
The women are nameless,
the children sexless, their relations
to the men unexplained.

We are not supposed to think
about a song they might have been singing,
about a bite of melon dissolving in a mouth,
about the words that were their last,
about the moments between impact and death.
We are not supposed to think
about the cost—four innocents.
We are not supposed to think.

Tasting the Fruit from the Tree of the Knowledge of Good and Evil at the Stop and Shop in Boston

Take a bite of this apple,
a Braeburn from Washington.

Taste rain of small particulates blown from China,
decades of windfall decomposed to humus,
shower of blossom and petal drift,
shroud of pesticide, the picker's cough
like pebbles in the throat.
Taste sweat wiped from his brow,
his breath held underwater while searchlights swept,
while rifle shots riffled the Rio Grande.
Taste Sonoran Desert dust tramped north,
dollars sent south, the mail's slowness,
the hunger of waiting, then finally,
corn, beans, rice,
mirrored meals of the split family.

Take another bite.

Taste the cool dark hold
of the eighteen-wheeler, the driver's
breath: coffee, cigarettes, sleeplessness,
and sleep stolen on off-ramps, truck engine running,
carbon monoxide released to air,
the song of wheels on transcontinental asphalt,
the crossing of mountains, prairies, corn fields.
Taste the escaping fumes as the truck's tank is filled,
Taste frigid arctic water
where the drill pulls crude from the deep shelf.
Taste the caribou grazing

beside the long snake of the pipeline.
The northern forests burning, the ice caps melting.

This apple from the picker's hand
to yours, a continent away.
Taste the sweetness and ruin.

In Oklahoma 2016

They are giving up
the illusion of solid ground.
Boom! tremble. Boom! tremble.
As if below the surface, something large
shouts and shakes itself awake.
Nineteen quakes last week.
More than nine hundred last year.

For millions of years, in the cracked
crust of earth's bedrock—pressure
building along the faults, the slip
of release. Eons of salt water intrusion,
sediment settled, hardened, rift, uplift,
erosion. The slow dance of geology.

Shale layers compressed from an ancient sea
are packed with a cache of oil and gas,
pulled up now to fuel the human machine.
Salt water releases too from that rock,
briny and toxic, useless—pumped
back into earth below aquifer,
below shale extraction layers.

Pumped deep into the Arbuckle, porous
layer of sandstone, limestone, dolomite
just above bedrock. Millions of gallons
a day as if its capacity were infinite.
Now water creeps into faults,
speeds the dance to frenzy,
sends to the shaking surface
its message: Boom! Enough!

Unknown Arts

in memoriam Challenger astronauts, January 28, 1986
[Daedalus] turned his thinking toward unknown arts, changing the laws of
nature.
                                                    —Metamorphoses, *Ovid*

Ignition and so much thrust
slowly, slowly overcame gravity.
Inside, they were heavy with its pull.
Above the fire that lifted them to lightness,
they rode off on a rocket trail,
confident as cowboys.

Just before they disappeared,
the straight path out of this world
veered and burst into arcing chaos,
a flash too fast to comprehend,
a momentary pyre.
They plummeted into the sea.

They were gone
before the ballyhoo died into silence,
before grief edged in
from a sky obscenely serene.
A disembodied voice named it
"a major malfunction."

We see them out there still,
our unburied dead,
out where we have sent them,
out where we have soared
in our imaginations,
weightless as their ashes.

The Plague of Squirrels

Hundreds are dead on the road
from Kennebunk to Boston,
hundreds alive in the trees
storing nuts against shortage.

They scurry over the attic floor,
fingernails scraping slate.
I dread the sound of their quarrels,
the hard warning of hoarding.

They are lean and desperate,
watching the dwindling acorn supply
and the wind-ruffled tails of the dead
killed in their frenzy to forage.

I wonder how to prepare.
I dream of red rivers.

Better That

It's seals that bring to shore the great white sharks
and seals we think are like us. They gather
keening at the bar, while a lone shark lurks

just below the surface past the breakers,
waiting always for the moment to strike,
thrust that turns the sea to bloody lather.

We do not think instead we might be like
these stalkers—dangerous, predatory,
driven by hunt and hunger, day and night,

circling. Like them are we solitary,
given to constant restless motion? Yet,
better that than something ordinary.

Much better that than prey. Let's not forget
how often we attack without regret.

Outer Reach

Stun of lightning. Rip of thunder.
All night storms chase each other
over this narrow curl of land.
Each time, we startle awake
in the unfamiliar bed in a room
high on the edge of the scarp.
We stand naked at the window
looking over the sweep of harbor
to the lights of Provincetown
refracted in drop-spattered glass.

The power goes. Darkness.
No sound but storm percussion
and susurration of wind in pines.
The glass fogs. The air grows thick
with our co-mingled sweat and breath
and something we haven't named
sitting heavy in the room.
We open the door to riot,
stand in the drenching.
In the strobe of lightning,
your face. Light. Dark.

We sleep and wake to a day
calm and bright—except,
from beyond the dune,
the voice of the riled sea.
Outside in cleansed air
and steady light, I see
that all has changed.

Couple

I listen for the other shoe
to fall. Nothing. I find you

sitting on the edge of our bed,
shoe in hand, holding your head,

waiting like me, to see
what words we'll speak

this last night before parting
each of us still smarting

from imagined slights.
Be still. Turn out the lights.

In the dark, face to blind face,
we might finally move toward grace.

Journey

Look out the bright window,
then close your eyes.
There is the window dark,
frame light. Two negatives
make a positive.

We can begin again.
Try to be positive,
watching the endless
yellow line on the highway
crossing Kansas.

Where are we
going crisscrossing
the continent, crossing
each other at every cross
roads? We are not lost.

Haven't I shown you
the magic of photo
negative on eyelid?
(And other wonders
I won't mention.)

Except to say,
try to remember
everything equally.

Arithmetic 1952

If there are 13 first graders
and 16 second graders enrolled
in the one-room schoolhouse
plus 1 teacher
who comes in early
to wash the chalkboard
while heat clangs
into the radiators,
how many people belong
in the one-room schoolhouse,
boys and girls?

We copy numbers from the board:
$13 + 16$. $(6 + 3 = 9; 1 + 1 = 2)$.
There are 29 children enrolled
in the one room schoolhouse
plus 1 teacher:
$(9 + 1 = 10)$ carry the one,
$(2 + 1 = 3)$: 30 people belong
in the one-room schoolhouse.

Today Billy Steffen is absent.
From the thirty people who belong
in the one-room schoolhouse
with two grades and one teacher,
we take away one for Billy.
We learn we can't take away
Billy from zero, so we borrow
one from three and take away
Billy from ten equals nine
and the three is two because
we borrowed one from it

equals twenty-nine people
in the one room schoolhouse.

Every day for weeks, we borrow
and take away one for Billy
who is still absent until one day
Teacher tells us Billy died of something
that multiplied. We don't know risky
multiplication. We only know
we are always thirty take away
Billy equals twenty-nine now.

In the one-room schoolhouse,
we will never add and carry the one
of Billy even though Billy is the one
we carry every day the rest of the year.

Brother

He played guitar by ear,
any tune we sang him.
And improvisations,
sweet like leaves rustling,
sounds that soothed him
and us—until
one day he threw away
the guitar.

I learned the thing
about land mines
is they surprise you
long after the war ends
when you are walking
on the usual path,
maybe through your own field
where you have walked for years,
but this is the day when
your foot finds the trigger.

Just as now, years after he jumped
from the moving car and ran off,
years after so many ruined visits,
everyone on edge, years after
I stopped answering his calls,
a guitar riff flattens me.

Walking the Wrack Line

Sometimes, I move
toward something far off,
barely visible, not yet
resolved into a nameable thing.
My mind tells stories:
Seal, dead or resting.
Seaweed. Driftwood.
The jacket lost in Portugal.
My father's fedora.

I hold back,
not wanting to come upon
a mangled seal or memory,
something better buried.
Wanting instead a delight—
the sea's surprise of shell or glass.

Beside me the ocean
heaves and settles.
I think of all
that is out there,
depths I can't plumb.
Maybe my brother's mind
is down there somewhere.

Lessons in Dying

Maples go early,

an easy
      blazing
            surrender.
Flamboyant,
     they toss
           crimson-gold
tokens,
     one by
          one,

to the soft azure sky.

      Oaks wait.
     November,
they burnish and hold.
Thin as paper, they rattle into March,
   still stubborn and tough.
    They're driven off
   on the last bitter
   wind before
    sap
      runs,
   a grudging
         surrender
  to the insistent
       whisper:

Make room.
     Make room.

after Emily Dickinson

A Darkness darts across the Path--
Illusion in the Dust—
Above—the Hawk whose Shadow cast
This Image we can't trust.

In midday sun—the Light transforms
The Hawk above in Flight—
Below—a startled scurrying—
A Darkening of Light—

The Soaring—all its Lightness takes
Its Darkness it casts down—
Yet cannot ever leave the One—
That follows on the ground.

One Summer

On solitary aimless walks,
he rambles out in rolling fields,
slingshot protruding from his pocket.
He studies flights of sparrows, crows,
smoothly moving the V, sighted
on a single bird. He does not shoot,

but tests his aim on tin cans, dandelions.
He lies in summer grass, watching clouds
gather into Goliaths beyond his range.
By September, he can hit a milkweed pod
from thirty feet, sending seeds
adrift on hot dry wind.

His neighbor's yard is full of targets.
One daisy in a profusion of dozens,
hit directly on the yellow bull's eye,
explodes petals that fall in flutters.
Across the lily pond, a slender stem
holds out to him, a single reddish bud.

This evening, he will overhear her—
It was a century plant about to open.
I won't live to see another blooming.
He will stow the slingshot in a drawer.
He will not follow, with the dead eye
of innocence, flights of birds.

But now, knowing nothing of centuries,
knowing only abundant time and targets,
he takes steady aim, releases his final
perfect shot, cleanly nips the bud,
starts at the swirl of keening marsh birds,
at his own terrible precision.

Nacirema Farm, August 18, 2011

When the old black cat
died at 3:13 AM,
they were awake,
and there was already a grave
dug for the old dog
who was supposed to die
last week,
but didn't.
She heard a horse whinny,
went to the barn for comfort,
stood in the yard speaking
to the stars, asking the animals
who had gone before
to come for the cat.

In the morning,
they drank coffee
and dug a small grave,
saving the larger one
for the dog who *would* die soon.
They washed the old cat's bed,
fed the living,
mucked the horse stalls.
The balm of necessity.

Postcard Not from Santorini

Just so you know,
this is not where I really am.
Where I am is less
picturesque—dry and barren,
with olive and almond trees
bent away from the relentless
etesian wind that blows
for days at a time, sending
dust through the cracks
and howling around corners.

I have learned a little
Greek, and how to harvest almonds
on the steep terraced hillside
by poking a long pole into the tree
so nuts fall onto a tarp.
Also, how to sit for long hours
at a rickety table outside a café
overlooking the hills
and the sea a half mile away.

How to drink thick coffee
slowly from a small cup
with a lot of other men
who don't know me
but accept me now
after so many months.
They pull their caps low
over their faces and stare
at whoever passes by,
the only sound
the click of worry beads
like a rosary—but different.

I know the spiky shells
of the horse chestnuts
have cracked open,
leaving the bronze nuts
with their pale faces
all over Bond Street sidewalk.
Remember how Janie kept
them until they shriveled,
how we found her stash
strewn among the toys
after she was gone?

Just so you know,
I won't be coming home.
This wizened wind-blasted island
is as good a place as any.

At the Island Market

inspired by Guadaloupe Queen, a painting by Mary Nickerson

Under a bleached sky, orange
umbrellas cast glowing shade
over fruit the colors of sunrise,
papaya, pineapple, mango.

Through waves of sweet and heat,
a woman glides like the ocean orisha,
flowing like slow water in her night-sea
dress blooming with moon flowers.

She chooses the nightshade eggplant
for its cool skin shining dark,
for the moon-white disks
that will open under her knife.

The sea shimmers in the distance
like someone beckoning.
Her gaze lifts and glazes.
She drifts toward home.

*The ocean orisha, Yemaya, is a goddess in the
Yoruba pantheon and is worshipped
in the Caribbean in various religions derived
from practices brought by African slaves.*

Eclipse

Bright night dims.
Our usually cool moon,
aloof mover of water and blood,
beacon for hunter and lover,
slowly smolders red.

Oh how we love
to humanize the moon,
see her face turned to us
like a blessing, not a cooled
circling stone from First Fire.

We know universal
geometry, predictable
axis and angle, know
this is not an omen,
dire or sublime. Still,

we feel the urge to chant,
dance naked on a precipice
arms outstretched
toward this blood sister
blushing behind our shadow.

What They Feared

Don't throw a leg
over the back of a horse
and gallop.
You might burst your hymen.

Don't wrap your legs
around the belly
of a djembe.
You might fry your eggs.

Ride like a lady.
Drum like a lady.
Sidesaddle.
Keep your knees together.

When a woman rides
bareback, wind whipping her
hair, the hard muscle
of horse surges beneath her.

When she holds a djembe
tight between her thighs,
her hands on the head
thrum the root chakra.

Oh yes, oh yes yes,
this is what they feared.

The Queen

Of course I'm angry. I'm betrayed
by my own huntsman,
bringing a boar's heart, not hers.
I'm obsessed with a mirror,
always looking for chin hairs,
crow's feet, gray locks. *I* was
the beauty who married the king.

What did I know?

Snow White. So white.
Those fool fawning dwarfs.
Everyone drooling over her
pale insipid prettiness.
She is all *It* now.
She thinks she'll marry
a prince, live happily ever after.

What does she know?

Take Princess Diana, shut up
in the Windsor Prison, eating
and throwing up, having pretty
boy babies, while the Prince
screwed his mistress. Until still
beautiful, she's dead in a tunnel.
They love her. Still. Beautiful.

What did she know?

Mirror, mirror, I want it back.
I see how they all look

through me now.
I remember the thrill
of my own beauty reflected.
You think I was not seduced
by their dreams of me?

Against Quickness

Not everywhere, not
in the hundred-yard dash,
the base runner stealing home,
peregrine plunging,
cheetah charging,
not in the hospital ER,
where a heart is restarted.

But don't give me the quickie,
quick oats, instant coffee, instant
message, short cut,
fast food in the fast lane.
No aerobic pace
to quicken the heart
in order to slow it.

Let me stand in the kitchen
coffee brewing, oats steaming
a scent that sends me to read again
The Cinnamon Peeler's Wife.
Let me lie a long afternoon
with a lover, dallying,
skins scented with spice.

Let me take the back road,
the slow road, stop
at a diner for lunch, wait
at the counter for pie
to come from the oven.
Let me ask for the recipe.
Let her write it longhand.

Let me meander the marshside,
stop for a kingfisher's darting chatter,
for a heron's lift, regal and slow,
wingbeats like thoughts leaving.
Let me look up to a cloudless sky
opening out and out to vastness,
opening into breath.

Slow

Once I ran without gratitude
for ligament and muscle, synovial fluid, bone
all working in silent synchronicity.

Now, I am slow enough
to hear the songs or warnings
of catbird, crow, mockingbird,

to see the fox slink into grass,
the great blue heron swallow a fish,
the terrapin burrow an egg nest.

I breathe sweet honeysuckle
and beach rose, peppery Scotch broom,
tang of exposed tidal flats.

Slower still, another year, perhaps I'll see
each blade of marsh grass shift on the tide,
the rose open, the shadow slide across the road.

Riding the Air

Wanna fly, you got to give up the shit that weighs you down.
If you surrendered to the air, you could ride it.
—Song of Solomon, *Toni Morrison*

Stand on a high barren scarp
facing a wind that rises off the sea,
a wind strong enough to lean on.
Take from the satin sack
of vanity and remembrance:
cling of silk on skin
scent of sawdust
a fist to the jaw.

Hold each thing like a smooth marble,
clear and heavy, cool in your palm.
Roll each one off the cliff into the sea.
Then roll this moment, the hot wind
on your skin and the blue blue sea,
the last marble, away.

Feel the lightness,
loose limbs that carry nothing.
Lean until you lift,
like a kite or a gliding gull.
Surrender your empty self
to rising air.

Lecount's Hollow Beach

Wellfleet, Massachusetts

The sun rises crimson,
misshapen by heavy air.
A shimmering path
leads from here to there.
Engines of fishing boats
drone a guttural song.
Scolding terns hover.
Waves roll over stones,
the sound of rain.

This is the place
to scatter my dust,
to be carried
in early light
on wind and water
over the sunpath
to horizon's edge
and beyond.

Cast me
into the sounds of morning,
dirge of boat engines,
shore birds keening,
satiny rustle of waves,
silence,
stones shushing in surf,
silence.

Addressed to Herself

Lilies blare their orange trumpets
as if in your sixty-ninth year,
they might finally have
your undivided attention.

Bloom and fade.
Bloom and die.
It has taken you a long time
to get this message.

No longer driven
everywhere by lust and longing
wanting more and more of everything.
Now you know there is no doing

the undone. You will not run
a marathon or have a child.
You will not don red shoes
and dance for hours.

I know you miss the longing,
anticipation that something
unnamed and urgent is coming.
Here is what you have instead:

now and now and now.
This perfect summer day,
a song to all your senses.
Wind in pines, scent of jasmine.

The dancing lilies opening
their wild orange fanfare.

Moondial

At night in the woods
after snow piles deep
and the storm moves away,
the bare trees mark
time with their shadows
falling on moonlit drifts.

Sleepless, I watch
the spinning dance
of earth and moon
in the arcing light,
each trunk a gnomon
tracing the hours.

In the scrying bowl
of the full moon,
portent and memory
appear and vanish—
unreadable mysteries
that slip away at dawn.

The Cone of Uncertainty

Opening out from the spinning
cyclone symbol on the weather map
is the storm's possible path
widening to unpredictable.

Just as our futures widen
into all that could be ahead
surrounded by the vastness
of all that cannot.

At our births, within
our cones of uncertainty,
wars and weather, words
that might be spoken or withheld,

children and lovers, trains missed
or caught, shots fired, gardens tended,
kites and kitchens, fence and fire,
blossom and blight,

some moments of grace.

Until what is possible shortens and narrows.
Peace is out for this generation. Also the end
of hunger and travel to Mars or the far stars.

Which is why, even in the world's worst straits,
every birth begins a cone of hope.

The Last

There's one more bit of lobster on your plate,
butter-dipped, the very height of pleasure,
so rich and sweet you hold your fork and wait,
a tantalizing pause. You want to measure

this delight before it's done. Now the wine,
one sip left to savor, a pinot gris
that lingers on your tongue. Its taste reminds
of what is gone, of what is yet to be.

And now your lover's hand rests on your thigh.
You turn your mind from others in the past,
forget those other kisses, other sighs.
You believe you've saved the best for last.

In food and wine and love, this final test—
with all else gone, of course the last is best.

About the Author

Lucile Burt is a retired high school English and creative writing teacher currently living in Wellfleet, Massachusetts. Her poems have appeared in various small press journals and in the anthology *Teaching with Fire*. Several poems have been selected to be read for the "Poetry Sunday" segment on WCAI, the local NPR station. Her chapbook *Neither Created Nor Destroyed* won the 2012 Philbrick Poetry Prize from the Providence Athenaeum and was published in April 2012. The work of writing poetry, with its careful attention to sound and rhythm, is a kind of meditation that helps her see connections that might otherwise go unnoticed.